STEEL FRIEND

Save on Every Ton, Make More Profits, and Get
Right Quality - On Time, *Everytime*

YOUR STEEL FRIEND

Save on Every Ton, Make More Profits, and Get
Right Quality - On Time, *Everytime*

ANKIT MEHTA

Worldwide Publishing by
Pendown Press
Powered by Gullybaba

PENDOWN PRESS
Powered by **Gullybaba Publishing House Pvt. Ltd.,**
An ISO 9001 & ISO 14001 Certified Co.,
Regd. Office: 2525/193, 1st Floor, Onkar Nagar-A, Tri Nagar, Delhi-110035
Ph.: 09350849407, 09312235086
E-mail: info@pendownpress.com
Branch Office: 1A/2A, 20, Hari Sadan, Ansari Road, Daryaganj, New Delhi-110002
Ph.: 011-45794768
Website: PendownPress.com

First Edition: 2022
Price: ₹299/-
ISBN: 978-93-5554-316-5

All Rights Reserved
All the ideas and thoughts in this book are given by the author and he is responsible for the treatise, facts and dialogues used in this book. He is also responsible for the used pictures and the permission to use them in this book. Copyright of this book is reserved with the author. The publisher does not have any responsibility for the above-mentioned matters. No part of this publication may be reproduced, distributed, or transmitted in any form or by any means, including photocopying, recording, or other electronic or mechanical methods, without the prior written permission of the publisher and author.

Layout and Cover Designed by Pendown Graphics Team
Printed and Bound in India by Thomson Press India Ltd.

Dedicated to...

My Father, "Khushal Das Mehta", for always empowering me, for establishing Mehta Steels with strong foundations and clear directions of ethics and standards and for always encouraging me to achieve new milestones in my life and my career. He is my biggest inspiration, my motivator and my mentor.

*My Daughter
Namasvi Mehta–my lifeline.*

Contents

Foreword *by Aruna Sharma*	i
Foreword *by Anirban Dasgupta*	ii
Preface	iii
Acknowledgements	vii
Introduction	ix

Chapter 1
Understanding Steel and Steel Products — 1

Chapter 2
Understanding the Steel Trading Ecosystem — 6

Chapter 3
So, Who Buys Steel? — 9

Chapter 4
Should You Buy Steel on Credit? — 12

Chapter 5
The Right Way to Buy Steel! — 16

Chapter 6
Ethics vs Profits is a Myth! 20

Chapter 7
Do's & Don'ts to Ensure Profitability! Part 1 24

Chapter 8
Do's & Don'ts to Ensure Profitability! Part 2 28

Chapter 9
Rome wasn't Built in a Day: Neither is a Brand or Culture 32

Chapter 10
Honoring the Human Aspect of the Steel Industry 36

Chapter 11
Coping with Price Volatility 41

In Conclusion 45

Foreword

"His book 'Your Steel Friend' is based on his experience in running a steel related business with focus on process close monitoring and corrections to enable legitimate savings and thus add to earnings. Coming from hands on person makes it an interesting book."

– **Dr. Aruna Sharma**
*Practitioner Development Economist,
Ex Secretary Steel Government of India,
was Member RBI High Level Committee,
Publications UNDP, FAO*

Foreword

Shri. Ankit Mehta has shared his story of the trials and tribulations faced by him through his entrepreneurial journey spanning over two decades. His foray into diverse ventures, particularly his experiences in the steel enterprise is narrated cogently bringing out various aspects of the value-chain of the Steel Industry. Drawing from his learnings and practical experience, he has enunciated profit mantras that should prove invaluable to the readers.

I wish him the very best for his book- **"Your Steel Friend"** and his future endeavours.

– **Anirban Dasgupta**
Director I/c SAIL-Bhilai Steel Plant

Preface

Hi Friends, I am Ankit Mehta, the author of this book that you are holding in your hands. And it gives me great delight that this book has found you.

I am no magnate or tycoon, nor am I a management expert with big degrees to my name.

However, I assure you that I have something extremely valuable to share with you.

Between the covers of this book, you will find the tools, tips, techniques and profitability mantras that no business school teaches you and no successful business owner will share with you.

In my journey, beginning as a young entrepreneur and then joining my family business, Mehta Steels as a 2nd generation entrepreneur, I have observed and lived the pain points and challenges of the manufacturers, traders as well as buyers of the Steel industry.

I have experienced all stages of the value chain that is the backbone of this fraternity, and this book is the result of all my experiences and challenges, the failure, the road to recovery, the problem solving, the solutions and finally, my desire to share it all with others so that they may bypass the challenges that are universal to the Steel fraternity and may run an ethical and profitable business no matter what stage of the business cycle they may be at.

The sole purpose of writing this book is to share my learnings and experience that have evolved into expertise with others to benefit the fraternity as a whole.

How it all began

Mehta Steels was started by my Father, Shri K.B Mehta, in 1992 at Bhilai. We specialize in Steel trading activities, majorly dealing in finished Steel products such as Mild Steel Plates, Boiler Quality Plates, High Tensile Plates, Sail Hard Plates, Checkered Plates, Hr Sheets, Hr Coils, Iu Rails, Crane Rails, Ms Angles, Ms Beams, Ms Channels, Ms Flats, Ms Round, Ms Square, Ms Pipe, A Profile Crane Rails, Etc.

We supply these products Pan-India and export them across the globe as well.

After graduating in commerce from Sydenham College in Mumbai, I enrolled in MBA and simultaneously began my entrepreneurial journey, setting up my first business of manufacturing Binding Wires; where though I made mistakes, but I was successful, and then I integrated backwards and set up a manufacturing of HB Wires which are the raw material for Binding Wires and then the family decided to invest all their savings into setting up an Induction Furnace as setting up an Induction Furnace or a Sponge Iron unit as it was the trend those days in Bhilai & Raipur.

I was put in charge of this project, especially the raw material sourcing, and this allowed me to observe the scrap market and understand the iron and steel industry in depth. I understood the challenges and pain points of the manufacturers and also what the buyers feel and how they think.

Due to our lack of experience and knowledge in that field, we suffered significant losses on this project, and it had to be shut down. This was not merely a financial loss, it made me spiral into depression, and I left my home town and worked in a call center for a while. I have shared this aspect of my life journey in detail in the introductory part of the book.

However, as the wise say, challenges only make one stronger, and so it proved to be with me. My failures became my biggest learnings, egging me on to find solutions not just for myself but for others, collectively as a whole. Like the fire of furnaces forges and shapes soft iron ore into strong Steel, so the fire of challenges and failures forged me into the strong and flourishing entrepreneur and the person I am today.

And I am choosing to share that journey and its precious learnings with you to help catapult your business to the zenith of success and profitability.

The truths shared in this book are not of the loud, disruptive kind. Instead, they are small, simple and subtle shifts. But believe me, the impact they bring you will begin to be visible almost immediately.

I have ensured that the language of the book is conversational and easy to understand and that the tools, techniques and mantras are easy to implement.

This book will prove valuable for almost everyone in the value chain in the Steel fraternity, be it manufacturers, traders, fabricators or buyers or even those who are part of the sales force of any Steel company. Also, this book will add value to your operations no matter whether you are a new entrant to this industry or an established player.

So friends, use the sharings in this book, apply them to your life and business, make them your lifestyle and see where your journey goes, for I believe that "Mazaa journey me hi hai, the journey is indeed the destination. And my personal realization is that as we involve and evolve with our MOA (Our potential customer) & the market, our MOA also evolves.

As our lens evolves, we as humans evolve and our viewpoint changes. It's fun to see these transformations occurring through the lens of life..."

So happy journey to success and profitability, friends, and enjoy the journey. ***Journey ka mazaa lo doston...***

And let's dive in straightaway...

Wishing you success as long-lasting and strong as Steel

Your Steel Friend

Acknowledgements

First and foremost, I would like to thank my parents, who gave me abundant love and a nurturing environment during my childhood. That enabled me to be self-confident and independent.

My Brother Pratik Mehta for always being by my side and empowering me with freedom and support, which is unparalleled. With immense patience, he absorbs and takes into his stride the tantrums I throw at times; he is not just a partner in our company, he is an equal partner in all my success.

I want to thank Anshul Goel of Brahma Gems for triggering in me the thought of writing a book a year back and for giving me that initial confidence to start the process of writing the book when I was stuck in taking even the first step.

I would like to thank Akshar Yadav for being a great mentor; though I have not been able to attend any of his classes, his teachings have been influential.

I am very thankful to Dinesh Verma, CEO of Pendown Press and his team for their support and suggestions during the creative process.

Last but not least, I would like to thank my wonderful wife, Jinal Mehta, for being a constant pillar of support and encouragement throughout the process. This book and this journey would not have been possible without you – I love you.

"Mazaa Journey me hi hai......." – Ankit Mehta

Introduction

Who am I, and what do I do?

I am an entrepreneur not only by passion but also by birth because I was born into a Gujarati Vaishnav family. Since childhood, I consistently witnessed my Father working tirelessly with dedication in his Steel Trading Business. I started accompanying him to the office during school vacations ever since I was in class 9th. That is when I came into close contact with Steel products and the Steel industry.

So, Steel literally runs in my blood!

As far as academics go, I hold a Bachelor of Commerce (B.Com) degree from Mumbai University. I tried pursuing my MBA too from a local college. Unfortunately, 80% attendance was mandatory to pass the course in those days. This proved challenging for me, as I was also starting my entrepreneurial journey at that time.

I was building my first Binding Wire Factory, and when the conflict of interest between academics and industry arose, I chose industry as I felt my real learning would be on the field. After much deliberation between classroom learning and on-the-job, hands-on learning, I went with the practical learning method and started working on my Binding Wire Factory project. I was instrumental in the complete set-up, production and trading of Binding Wires.

After this, I decided to integrate backwards by setting up a unit of HB Wires. After this, I was instrumental in setting up an MS Ingot Unit or Induction Furnace as it is commonly known, which eventually went into heavy losses and had to be shut down. Though the losses were heavy, the learning was massive too. It left me with a lot of helpful experiences.

I then established a Sheet Fabrication unit, and I realized that my true core is Steel Trading, as it is something I know inside-out.

Using all my efforts and learning from past experiences, I began offering my customers alternative and realistic cost-saving products; thus, I was able to add real and immense value to their lives.

Tough Times don't last. Tough People do!

When I look back on my entrepreneurial journey, it is difficult not to recall the losses and the sense of failure that I was drowning in then.

Losing my first business baby, my Binding Wire factory, was a complete nightmare. My loss was compounded by the loss of my HB Wire Unit to large-scale manufacturers. Then I lost the Induction Furnace, too, all at a very young age. Getting over these heavy losses was truly hard, especially after losing the Furnace. I began to believe that everything I associated with turned out to be a failure.

I decided to step back a bit to recover from this and get an objective view of things. I took a break of 6 months and moved to Pune. There I worked at a Call Center and took voice & accent training. During my free time, I started learning about Insurance and Business processes and finding customers for Finished Steel Products. This proved to be the turning point. It all began to change from here. I could finally make sense of all the hardships I had faced earlier.

After intensive research into success processes, many years of experience and having turned around my business through systemized planning today, I can say that I completely understand the pain points of the customers using Steel Products.

Being able to relate to the customers' challenges from varied perspectives and roles as Purchaser, Owner, Project Manager, Manufacturer etc., has given me a clearer understanding of all issues. This has helped me develop the best processes for customer interaction and customer delight and provide solutions to these challenges. As a result, today, I am catering to Binding, HB, Induction and Fabrication Units for their in-house Steel requirements.

My journey began in 2003, and for nearly two decades now, I have worked with 1000s of clients and helped them achieve massive profits and eliminate losses.

I feel blessed and fortunate to be sought after and respected by my clients and peers in the industry. The reason for my credibility is because they know that I have been through hardships and struggles of various Steel making processes and thus relate to their concerns and needs genuinely and offer them authentic and ethical solutions for saving money on their Steel procurements.

The Challenges

If done right, the Steel industry is very lucrative. However, the current scenario in this industry has its typical set of challenges, such as:

- High Capital Industry (Capital Intensive Industry)
- Dominated by Deep Pocket Players
- High Competition (Due to a High Number of Players)
- High Freight Costs
- High Processing Times
- Off-The-Shelf Availability

However, over the years, I have developed proven techniques and adopted some mantras to overcome these challenges completely and stay one step ahead in the game always.

In the coming chapters, I will share all of these with you in detail so that you, too, will be able to flourish and multiply your profits and strengthen your reputation as a passionate and ethical player in the industry.

This book will not only help you become profitable, but it will also help you build better working relationships with your vendors, customers and peers.

So, let's deep dive into it without further ado.....

Chapter 1

Understanding Steel and Steel Products

To excel and be profitable in any business, it is always best to begin with the basics. So, let's first take a brief look at Steel and its various products and usages.

The Source

Steel, as most of us are aware, comes from Iron Ore. Iron Ore is found as mineral deposits in mines at specific geological sites. The quality of Iron Ore found in India is pretty good.

Iron Ore is excavated from the mines and processed and purified through various methods. It can be done either through a Blast Furnace or by Pelletization through the DRI method, where it is turned into Direct Reduced Iron or Sponge Iron as it is commonly called.

When Iron Ore is excavated, the Iron content is about 60%; however, it can be purified up to 90% through the DRI method.

It is then further purified up to 99%. No matter what purifying process is used, Iron Ore ends up being melted. However, it is of no use in its liquid form. It is cooled and molded into various shapes and sizes and formed into products that are widely used.

Steel Products: A Wondrous Universe

The cooled Iron Ore product that the purification process finally brings is referred to as Mild Steel (MS).

When MS is shaped into products, they are called Semi-rolled or Cast products. These products can be in the form of These:

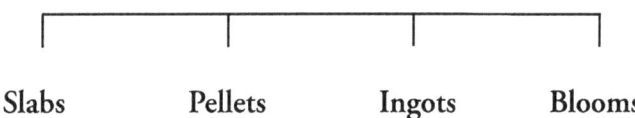

Slabs　　Pellets　　Ingots　　Blooms

These products can further be rolled out into structural Steel sections, which can be further classified into

1. Long Products
2. Flat Products

Long products are long steel sections that come in various shapes and sizes and are used in a variety of projects.

1. Long Products

Rails

These can be of two types, Track Rails and Craned Rails. Track Rails, as the name suggests, are used as Train Tracks. While the Craned Rails are different in shape, thickness and strength, Craned Rails can bear loads as heavy as 100-160 Tons.

MS Angles

These are L-shaped Steel sections. They can be of equal or unequal flanges. When the two flanges are of the same length, they are called L ANGLES. They are usually anywhere between 25 MM-250 MM.

When the two flanges are unequal, it is called an UNEQUAL ANGLE. These angles are used for space and design in specific engineering processes.

I Beams

These are very popular products. They are also commonly referred to as columns, pillars or beams. They come in I & H forms. They come in various international profiles such as ISMB, IPM, HEA, HEB, IPP, WPP, UB, UC, NPB etc. In the Indian market, Beams are usually from 80 MM to 900 MM.

MS Channels

Also known as C-CHANNELS (In American sizes). ISMC, UPE, UPN are European specifications. The Indian Standard for MS Channels is 75-100 MM. MS Channels are widely used in building and infrastructure, especially in high rises.

MS Flats

Also known as Pattis, these are used in gate, grill designs and automobiles. They can usually measure anywhere from 18 MM to 500 MM and are a mass-use product.

TMT

Also known as Sariya or Rebars, it is perhaps the most popular product in the Indian scenario and is used widely in the civil construction industry. They measure from 6 MM to 40 MM.

Wire Rods & Wire Coils

These are used both as raw materials and as finished products. They can be drawn into MS WIRES, BINDING WIRES, GI WIRES and WIRE NAILS. There is a lot of value addition that can be done with the aid of this product.

MS Rods

Also known as MS ROUNDS, these are 'O' shaped pipe-like structures ranging from 6 MM to 130 MM. It's very heavy and also referred to as XL. They have plain surfaces free of any ribbing.

MS Square Rods

These are mainly used in gates, grills, and cranes. Heavy 50 × 50 or 60 × 60 MM rods are used in cranes. These are available from 8 MM to 60 MM.

2. Flat Products

MS Plates

These come in various qualities defined by grades. They are of three types, PRIME or STRUCTURAL QUALITY Plates specified as IS 2062 E-250 BR, BOILER QUALITY, or BQ Plates are heat resistant plates used in turbines and boilers or other high-pressure applications, and HIGH TENSILE PLATES or HT Plates as the name suggests, are plates with high tensile strength and load-bearing capacity.

HR Coils & Sheets

These are rolled coils with thicknesses ranging from 1.5 MM to 25 MM and widths ranging from 800 Mts to 2.5 Mts. Using the Decoiler route or Coil cutting route, these coils can be cut into sheets of desired sizes.

Checkered Plates

These plates are a little raised with a checkered pattern on the surface compared to other plates. This helps in durability and grip and is thus used in floor beds.

With such a wide variety of products available, there are immense opportunities for value additions. Also, as an entrepreneur, there are various possibilities for forward and backward integration to design your business profitably.

Chapter 2

Understanding the Steel Trading Ecosystem

To be profitable in any industry, it is essential to understand that particular industry completely. Now that we have gained an understanding of the multidimensional universe of Steel products, let's also delve into the ecosystem of Steel trading.

Based on their activities, reach, and abilities, there are many sorts of classifications possible for the players in the Steel industry. Here is an introduction to all of them.

The Retailers

These are the shops that you see in and around your neighborhood most commonly. They are the immediate choice for smaller quantities of Steel products. They mostly stock long products, the Sariyas (TMTs) & pattis being the major ones and some flat products such as thin sheets like gp sheets, cr sheets, hr sheets, wire nails etc.

The Stockists/Wholesalers

These are the traders who buy materials from Steel Mills and stock a large inventory of a wide variety of products. These stockists hold and maintain inventory for long periods to be able to cater to their customers immediately on demand. They have products available in all grades and a range of thicknesses.

These stockists can also be masters of certain products as my company specializes in MS Plates, Rails, and Structural Steel products.

The Steel Manufacturers

These are the plants that manufacture the products; they are large in size. Their operations are volumetric based and focused on giving maximum output in minimum time to maintain profitability.

The Steel Suppliers

These are traders who do not invest in stock and do not hold any inventory. Still, they are connected to various manufacturers and wholesalers and collect material from various places and supply it to the customer whenever they receive orders. Steel suppliers often extend credit to customers.

Advantages of Stockists V/S Manufacturers & Suppliers

Since manufacturers are volume-based, they have their limitations and supply only one kind of product in one container/vehicle, which one may not need in such large quantities. While stockists like us do not have this limitation, they can supply various products in one vehicle. For example, they can bundle up a ton of sariya with 5 tons of 5 types of angles or anything else in one vehicle, saving resources for the customer.

The advantage stockists have over suppliers is that they can supply the material instantly due to their large and varied inventories saving the customer a delay in their project, which in turn saves money.

Also, unlike retailers, stockists can supply large quantities of materials on-demand and also a variety of materials in one place. This saves the customers time and money because they do not need to go from one place to another to find what they need.

Agents

In addition to the above classifications in the Steel ecosystem, there is one more vital participant, the agent. These agents or brokers are the matchmakers that bring vendors and customers together for their mutual benefit. These agents have been a tradition in the industry and are used as safe, fair and neutral buffers even while doing business with friends to keep things professional.

These agents generally operate on a really low margin, but they play a very critical role in the industry.

Whether you are a manufacturer, trader or supplier, with this chapter, I'm sure you have a better understanding of all the roles. This chapter and this understanding are especially helpful and necessary for new entrants into the industry and also for customers in deciding who is the best-suited vendor for them.

Chapter 3

So, Who Buys Steel?

Now that we have a better understanding of Steel Products and the players in the Steel industry let's understand who buys Steel.

Buyers from within the Fraternity

Now the interesting thing here is that there is an overlap between the players and the customers in the Steel industry.

Within the Steel industry itself, there are three main categories of customers:

- **The Agents:** (Who buy and supply on demand)
- **The Traders:** (Those who hold large stock or lesser stock for retail purposes)
- **The Manufacturers:** This might sound surprising, but yes, the manufacturers are customers too because they buy it in the form of raw material and then add value to it and create finished products. For example, they might be buying Iron Ore and then making ingots out of it or finished products such as binding wires.

Buyers from within the Fraternity

Apart from these Steel fraternity buyers, there are external buyers too; in fact, there exists a whole value-chain that works day and night tirelessly with unending zeal and enthusiasm, such as:

Steel Fabricators

Sheet Metal Processors

Heavy Machinery/Equipment Manufacturers: That make equipment such as Forklifts, EOT Cranes, Gantry Cranes and all other sorts of cranes, or material handling products such as Coco-1, Behemoths, and Monsters etc. There is a vast variety of products in which it is used.

Any New Entrant To The Industry: Will always be a buyer, to begin with.

Customers can be B2B or B2C, or both.

Builders & Contractors: All buildings need Steel in one form or another, such as Sariyas, pattis etc.

The Infrastructure Sector: All bridges, roads, over bridges, tunnels, metro projects, and railways require steel and steel products in myriad forms. The infrastructure buyers can be either Government Institutions or they can be private sector operators.

Heavy & Capital Intensive Industry: Most capital-intensive heavy industries, such as Cement & Sugar plants, require steel and steel products in significant quantities.

Retail Customers: These are mostly people who are constructing a home, office and, of course, any other building.

In this first section of the book, you have thoroughly acquainted yourselves with the Steel industry, the sources of purification, the types, the products, the players, the buyers and the challenges.

In the next chapters, you will learn how to create more profits and ease in the Steel industry and thrive in this ecosystem.

Chapter 4

Should You Buy Steel on Credit?

I am sure many of you make a practice of buying Steel and Steel products on credit. And many others wonder whether to go ahead and do so.

The answer is Noooooooooooooo!

If Steel is your bread and butter and the entire profitability of your project depends on it.

Then STOP BUYING STEEL ON CREDIT NOW!

Are You Really Smart?

Many businessmen feel that instead of financing themselves and buying Steel on cash from their vendors, it is smarter to buy it on credit and leverage the vendor's money to benefit their business.

But let me enlighten you, **you could not be making a bigger mistake than this.**

Here's the simple math behind it, which honestly sometimes makes me wonder why a businessman would be unable to understand it and keep making such a costly mistake.

A bank or any other financial institution usually lends us money at about 6-8% interest.

While buying on credit from the Steel fraternity, usually, it will be at least at a 12% markup.

Let's say you are buying a product at 50 Rs/Kg, and you say that you will pay tomorrow, it immediately goes up to 500 Rs. and if you say you will pay in 15 days' time, it jumps to 700 Rs. and if you want 30 days credit, you will end up at 1200 Rs/Kg.

Now you and I can both do the math and understand that it is an extremely high price to pay compared to other sources of finance. By buying on credit, you are actually losing a lot of money!

So think again and tell me, are you really being smart???

Despite being so damaging, most MSMEs keep making this fatal mistake.

If you want your business to be truly profitable, stop making this mistake of buying Steel on credit.

Instead, immediately after reading this, sit down with your accountant and your chartered accountant, work on your finances thoroughly and try to identify different ways and sources of getting funds to buy Steel in cash.

Become Privileged!

Till now, I have only talked about the massive profitability you make by saving on interest when you stop buying Steel on credit. But there are other advantages to buying in cash too.

Now once you become cash-rich and tell your vendor that I will pay you in advance, you immediately become a liquid resource to them and hence a favorite with them. They give you preferred status because they don't want to annoy you. And what benefits exactly this preferred status brings, you might ask.

Well, for one, your deliveries will be quicker, the vendor will never delay your delivery, and this will reflect in your business cycle too. You, in turn, will be able to deliver quickly to your customers and thus get payments faster. This will reduce your cash cycle significantly.

Secondly, since you are a preferred customer and the vendor doesn't want to lose your business, you can be assured that they will always deliver quality material to you.

Drive the Prices!

Also, when you pay in cash and the vendor doesn't want to lose you ever, then you have the upper hand. In such a scenario, you can drive and dictate the price you buy at. This leads to extra savings for you, which translates into more profitability.

Credit can damage Your Operations Too

Once you get into the habit of buying on credit, your psyche deems it as normal, so when your clients ask you for credit, you find it normal. Thus you become a victim of credit on both sides, and your Cash cycle is adversely affected.

Stay away from selling on credit. Instead, focus on selling the advantages of quality and value addition to the products. Selling on credit can sour your relationship with your client when it comes to recovery, but offering them value addition, quality and timely delivery will always keep you in their good books and keep them coming back.

Also, when we buy on credit, sometimes we extend ourselves beyond our limits. As clients keep giving us orders, we keep getting more material on credit to fulfill those orders, and we don't realize how much debt we are under. Once we are overextended, we become stressed, and that affects our entire operations.

When we buy on credit, we are always worried about how to pay back, and we keep running from pillar to post to arrange for the money. This leaves us with no time to scale up our business and invest time in research, new product and business development, and our business begins to stagnate.

The Profitability Mantra
Do Not Buy Steel On Credit!
This is an unfailing profitability mantra. If you adopt this mantra, I assure you that you will be profitable and will be able to see the difference in just 3 months.

Chapter 5

The Right Way to Buy Steel!

You are Throwing Money Away!

Reading the title of this chapter, I am sure you must be wondering what the meaning of this is. Buying Steel is buying Steel, so what could be wrong with it?

Well, the answer is there could be a lot wrong with the way you buy Steel for your project or organization.

To begin with, let's walk through how most people buy Steel.

You need Steel, so the first thing you do is shoot a mail to anywhere between 5-10 vendors stating your requirement and asking for the price. Or you send out a WhatsApp blast to your vendors stating your requirement and asking for quotes.

Right??? This is the common way of buying Steel!

However, let me tell you that there is nothing right about this way of purchasing Steel/Steel Products.

Once all the quotations are in, you check the prices and most often choose the one that is the lowest and place your order.

End result: You are very happy with yourself for having saved money by buying at the best price.

Sadly the reality is very different. You have actually thrown money away!

With a little more effort and out-of-the-box thinking, you could have saved a significant amount of money. But you threw that chance away. In fact, most of you don't even realize that such an opportunity even exists.

But that is the whole purpose of this book, to teach you techniques to be massively profitable in your steel business. So I am sharing below a powerful yet easy-to-use trick to buy Steel/Steel products the right and profitable way.

A Phone Call Can Save You Lots of Money!

If the amount of Steel you need to buy is a sizable amount of your operations, you must ensure that your procurement is profitable.

Say, for example, you need to procure 20 tons of Steel, and that is a sizable amount of your monthly volume of Steel, then don't just mail or WhatsApp your vendors. Pick up the phone and talk to them, if not all of them, then at least the top 5 of them. A phone call can work miracles and save you loads of money.

Tell your supplier about your requirement clearly, and state the purpose and amount. Ask them whether they can offer you something meeting your requirements at a discounted price.

When you personally make this effort to get in touch with your supplier, it is very likely that they will make more effort to help you in return.

- They could rack their brains and remember that they have a surplus stock of the nearest sections meeting your requirement and would be happy to offer them to you at a lower price than you would have paid for the product [even on the lowest quotation]. It is a win-win situation for both of you.

- They could also have some blocked/aged inventory that matches your needs, and they would again be happy to offer you at a bargain price, saving you loads of money on your procurement.

- It is also possible that they could suggest you an alternate cost-effective product that meets your requirements and thereby saves you money.

- In rare cases, if they are manufacturers, they might even be willing to re-engineer the product in a manner that is cost-effective without compromising on quality.

And Here's The Bonus

By talking to your supplier/s personally, you build trust both ways. You begin to value them for the efforts they are putting into making your procurement profitable.

And on the other hand, they give you the status of preferred customer as well because they perceive you as someone who is passionate about their business and only wants what is best for it at the best prices.

They begin to respect and admire your passion and dedication to your business. Whenever they have any cost-effective material or solution, they will undoubtedly think of offering it to you first.

Once you have firmly established this deep-bonded relationship with your supplier/s, then even a mail or WhatsApp message will get you the same beneficial results.

The Profitability Mantra

Personally call your supplier/vendor for your procurement at least once a month!

Try it with 5 suppliers or 1 supplier of every product and see the difference.

This is an unfailing profitability mantra. If you adopt this mantra, I assure you that you will be profitable, and this will prove to be a turning point in your business. You will be able to see the difference in just a few months.

Chapter 6

Ethics vs Profits is a Myth!

Myth vs Reality

Yes, you are reading it right! If you have ever been torn between choosing ethics or profits, then please know that this is like fighting with an imaginary enemy.

Because, in truth, ethics and profits are not choices where you need to choose either one or the other.

So the equation of

Ethics vs Profits is a Myth

The real equation is

Ethics = Profits is the Reality

The Unspoken Rule

In this chapter, we will address a very important topic, the role of ethics in the Steel fraternity.

Even though the Steel fraternity is very large and diverse, it is bound together by one unspoken rule:

All dealings must be ethical!

The entire industry stands as one unanimously on the role of ethics.

If you see and analyze the companies and organizations that have exhibited exponential growth in the Steel/Steel products industry, you are bound to notice that they have all been companies with an ethical approach to business.

So if you have ever been misguided into believing that the only way to profitability is turning a blind eye to ethics, please release this belief immediately.

Ethics can't be Faked

Let me bust another myth for you. It is impossible to pretend to be ethical and not be ethical in reality. It is not something that you can talk about or put up a show of being ethical. Where ethics are concerned, the wise old proverb "Actions speak louder than words" holds completely true.

Just saying "I am ethical" won't work. Ethics is a way of doing business and is reflected in all your business transactions. If you are truly ethical, it will show in your dealings with your customers, suppliers, employees, peers etc.

No Deviations Allowed

Also, if you are ethical, you are always ethical. It isn't a matter of choice and convenience. You cannot deviate even once. You can't say, "oh, this one time, it's OK not to be ethical; after all, I was ethical in all my last 10 transactions."

No! You cannot be, and you should not be unethical in even one single transaction!

The moment you deviate and indulge in even one unethical transaction, that very moment, you are creating the reason for your downfall.

That one single unethical transaction is enough to cause a dent in your reputation and business, way larger than the profit from that unethical transaction.

Even though it is a large fraternity, word travels at the speed of light in this fraternity, and before you even realize it, the news of your misdemeanor would be all over the fraternity.

Are you willing to be shamed for life for a momentary lapse in judgment? I am sure not!

Then don't let the lure of a quick buck drag you into a lifetime swamp of disrepute!

Build an Ethical Culture in Your Organization

All it takes is one WhatsApp message of an unethical transaction on a Steel fraternity group to report a company.

In today's digital age, the fraternity is strongly connected at all times of the day. So if anybody thinks that they can play dirty with a buyer or supplier and get away with it, they are sadly mistaken. When their deed comes to light, it will be difficult for them to survive in the Steel industry at all.

So friends, if you aspire to build a business empire in the Steel industry, you must first build a culture of ethical business dealings from the top down, starting with you.

Being ethical is beneficial as it inspires confidence in your employees too. It empowers your own team, and they will willingly vouch for you and your credibility in their interactions with suppliers or customers.

Ethical business behavior gives you a credible stand-in business circles and builds the foundation and platform for your business to grow exponentially in multiple dimensions.

And friends, ethical behavior should not be limited to just business, it should be an inherent part of your value system in all areas and all dealings of your life.

The Profitability Mantra

Build an ethical culture in your organization top-down and refrain from even one unethical transaction!

This is an unfailing profitability mantra. If you do not adopt this mantra, I assure you that you will never be profitable.

Chapter 7

Do's & Don'ts to Ensure Profitability! Part 1

The Mool Mantra

As a rule in the Steel industry, we always try to find the most economically priced Steel. To put it simply in Hindi, ***"Sabse sasta loha dhoondhte hain."*** Because we have to be competitive in this wide industry to thrive.

Here's the ***Mool Mantra***:

Ensure profitability in every single transaction, whether buying or selling.

We always focus on profitability while selling goods and often forget that another great way of being profitable is by saving costs. Therefore we must orient our efforts toward making our buying also as profitable as our selling.

When you focus on ensuring profitability on every ton of Steel that comes in or goes out of your business, you will never be at a loss. Rather you will enhance your profitability exponentially.

To ensure this, you must either negotiate personally with your vendors or set up fool-proof SOPs & systems to ensure profitable and quality buying even in smaller transactions because every ton you buy and every paisa you save adds up to your margins.

However, here is a special power tip for you.

Before you choose to get personally involved in a negotiation, carefully weigh whether the benefits received are worth spending your precious time and energy on it? Or could you be better off using that time and energy elsewhere in product or business development? Weigh whether the volumetrics justify your time, energy and involvement.

So how much did You Sell???

In our industry, the prime question is always, *"Kitna Maal Bechaa?"* Meaning, how much did you sell? Nobody asks how much did you earn? Nobody asks *"Kitna Kamaaya?"* This goes to show you that your earnings depend on how much you sell, and how much you sell is directly linked to how much you buy, so imagine, in addition to the profit you make on selling, if you could ensure profitability on every ton you buy how profitable you would be!

In simple words, this means that all our profits are linked to the quantities we deal in.

So making a profit on each transaction is very important. Make a habit of it.

Negotiate Better!

So negotiating better is the key to ensuring profitability on buying, and the keys to negotiating better are:

1. Volume
2. Cash

   1. **Volume:** When you buy in volumes, you not only become a preferred customer to your vendor, but you also save precious money on freight. Since Steel is a heavy material, it needs bigger and heavier vehicles to be transported.

      Thus if you order even smaller quantities, you still need to pay the whole rate for a full freight truck.

      Therefore it makes sense for you to order larger quantities at one go and get value for the entire payment for the truckload. Instead, if you order only half a truckload, you will still end up paying full freight, and you will lose money.

      Plan diligently and systematically for your project procurement.

      Work out the entire quantity of Steel needed for your project and order it in one go to avoid losing money through dead freight by ordering smaller quantities at different times.

      For certain industry-specific uses and fabrication purposes, your project might require different types of Steel/Steel products such as angles, plates, rods, sheets etc.

In such a scenario, find a vendor who can fulfill all your requirements and give you a truckload of varied types of material to avoid loss due to dead freight costs.

So always work out your entire requirement, club it together into truckloads, and then order in one go to save freight and ensure profitability instead of ordering in smaller lots and wasting money.

Also, when you buy larger quantities, you can reduce Scrap generation, and the more you optimize Scrap generation, the more you can enhance profitability. We will discuss this in detail later in the book.

2. **Cash:** That cash lets you negotiate better is something that everybody knows, and we have discussed it in detail in a previous chapter. *"Rokda Bolta Hai Boss"* means **"Cash Is King"**. It makes you a preferred customer and allows you to drive the price, thus making you profitable.

Chapter 8

Do's & Don'ts to Ensure Profitability! Part 2

The Dynamics of Buying Steel

In this chapter, I am sharing with you the rest of the tips to ensure profitability for your Steel Enterprise, and the way you buy Steel is an essential part of it.

We earlier discussed how the right price is critical in every buying transaction to ensure profitability. However, it is also very important to buy the right quality Steel for all your projects.

Your profitability is not driven only by the price and quantity of Steel you buy. There is another ingredient in the mix too. Getting the quality of the Steel right is crucial to the success and profitability of any project.

In certain projects, the technical requirements of the project are very specific and crucial. Such projects have specific needs for certain types or grades of Steel/Steel products, and these needs and specifications need to be adhered to and fulfilled strictly and completely.

For example, certain projects of the Indian Railways require Corten or corrosion-resistant material.

Therefore, if we want to do business seriously, we cannot indulge in casual buying or purchasing of materials. Just verbally calling up the vendor and saying, *"Yeh maal bhej do"* (send this material) won't suffice. Ensure that you specify exactly what type, grade or quality of material you need for your project in a clear and written communication through a detailed and specific Purchase Order.

This will help you successfully clear and pass all 3rd party inspection norms.

The Profitability Mantra

Along with the right pricing, ensure that you buy the right specification and quality of material as required by the project.

Price and Quality Specs are Interlinked

If you place the order for the correct quality of Steel right in the beginning, you can save on time and most likely on cost too. Let's understand this better through an example:

Suppose you order for XYZ material at an agreed-upon price, and then somewhere down the line, someone in your company then tells the vendor that they need a cut plate or cut size. Now, this is likely to add to your cost as well as time since your vendor isn't prepared for this. They haven't planned or scheduled themselves accordingly because you hadn't asked for this.

They will definitely ask you for additional money as they may need extra infrastructure and manpower to do this suddenly and urgently. Also, it will delay your delivery timeline because this wasn't scheduled.

Had you been careful about the specifications of your requirement beforehand, you could have driven and negotiated a better price. Now when you do it suddenly, the vendor gets the upper hand and has a bargaining advantage as you are stuck in the middle of your project.

The Profitability Mantra

Therefore, to ensure profitability, work out the specifications of your project carefully before ordering the raw material, or else you'll be stuck with surge pricing and extended delivery timelines mid-project.

Timely Delivery-Your Success Lifeline

In this evolving world, along with other things, the Steel industry has been witnessing revolutionary changes too. Talking specifically in the Indian context, earlier, we used to see the usage of mild Steel grades and traditional style Steel only. Today with the evolution of information technology, we are seeing the building and development of highly engineered infrastructure in and around us.

All such highly technical projects not only have stringent quality checks on material specifications, but these projects are highly time-sensitive, and they also have very tight delivery deadlines.

In most cases, there are very strict penalty clauses if you default on delivery deadlines.

Therefore, you must ensure that you choose a vendor partner who can support you with quality and timely deliverables. Also, you must ensure that you communicate your requirements clearly to them so that there is no confusion that could lead to delayed deliveries of material.

Another aspect of this timely delivery also includes ensuring timely and complete delivery of the order to even the remotest of locations.

Once you've accepted the order, remote locations or logistic challenges cannot be an excuse for delayed delivery.

For example, if there is a roof over bridge project in the middle of the jungle, that's a totally new development with no population for a 200 Km radius. If you fail to deliver on time or deliver short quantities, it can translate into major losses for the project and result in liquid damages, loss of further business and reputation for you. So, order on time and clearly, to deliver on time and completely.

The Profitability Mantra

Order your raw material on time so that you can deliver the products to your client on time. Communicate your order clearly to avoid confusion leading to a difference in quality or delay in delivery.

Chapter 9

Rome wasn't Built in a Day: Neither is a Brand or Culture

In this chapter, I will show you how to generate sales automatically without lifting a finger!

Yes, you heard me right. So, let's deep dive quickly...

Brand Identity

Friends, a critical tip to be profitable in the Steel industry is to create your own distinct brand identity.

A customer should be able to identify you easily and should want to do business only with you because they resonate with the identity and credibility you have established. This applies to every industry but especially to the Steel industry as it is an industry that survives and thrives only on trust.

Look around you; all the established **companies that are doing well are because they have created a USP or a Unique Selling Proposition for themselves.** They have established trust in the mind of the customer that they deliver what they claim. Also, **they have differentiated themselves by excelling in their products/services.** That is why the customer chooses them repeatedly.

Build a Culture of Excellence

In my many years of experience in the various trading and manufacturing aspects of the Steel industry, the most important factor that makes you the customer's preferred and first choice is the culture of your organization.

Believe me; you cannot force your customer to choose you. **That preferential treatment of being the top choice of your customer has to be earned.**

And that respect and choice are earned by creating a customer-centric and excellence-oriented culture in your organization.

And this customer-centric culture of excellence cannot be created overnight. It has to be introduced, nurtured and sustained right from the beginning and then has to be maintained by working on it every single day through our behavior in the organization.

Also, remember this culture will always flow top-down, so this has to begin with you. You will need to lead by example to instill this culture in your entire organization.

We at Mehta Steels ensure that we behave and perform in an ethical, Customer-centric and excellence-oriented manner. We ensure that we not only improve our company operations such as sales, marketing, product development, accounts etc., but we also improve our personal behavior with peers, colleagues, seniors, juniors, vendors, customers and just about everyone we interact with.

Compete with Yourself

We believe that before we compete with anyone else, we are our most fierce competitors. We encourage and challenge every individual in our organization to perform better on a daily basis.

We encourage each other to be better versions of ourselves every single day, bit by bit.

So, friends, when we try to improve daily bit by bit in our operations, processes, products, quality checks and interactions for and with our customers, it translates into a huge change; after all, Rome wasn't built in a day. Similarly, it takes work to build your organization's culture, brand and identity.

It will take time, be patient; as I said earlier, Rome wasn't built in a day!

Growth is the only constant in our lives; in order to survive and prosper, we must continue to grow on a daily basis. The moment you stop making efforts to grow, you become stagnant, and then you die!

The Profitability Mantra

One of the most important factors for any entrepreneur entering the Steel industry, in fact for any industry, is this:

Just as you review your turnover and profits daily, you must set up and review KPIs [Key Performance Indicators] for these excellence activities on a daily basis for the scope of improvement. This way, the culture of customer centricity & delivering excellence will become inherent to your team and your organization.

If you follow this profitability mantra completely and build a culture of customer-centricity and excellence and differentiate yourself from the other players in the industry, you will automatically generate sales. You will never have to chase customers; You will always be their preferred choice based on your culture and credibility!

Chapter 10

Honoring the Human Aspect of the Steel Industry

We are All Human

In the previous chapters, we have explored and discussed various aspects of the Steel industry, from making, buying, selling, types of products, transporting hacks, marketing secrets, Cost-saving techniques, maintaining quality, building an ethical culture, etc.

In this chapter, I am sharing with you a secret that will not only ensure profitability but also ensure that you will always be able to look yourself in the eye, in the mirror, with no burden on your conscience.

In this chapter, we will be talking about the human aspect of the Steel Industry.

In fact, what I am about to share shouldn't even have to be a secret or talked about at all. It should be our default way of being.

Yet many a time, we as human beings falter and fall short in our behavior toward other human beings. So, consider this a reminder to be kind and humane always and try to understand where the other person may be coming from and what trials they may be facing.

There is a Reason for Everything

People in the Steel industry are often perceived as rough, rugged, bordering on rude, loud-voiced and even arrogant at times. And yes, perhaps this perception is correct. We all enter this ecosystem, and this is the culture we see around us, and that is how we tend to become.

But now, the time has come to break this chain of behavior instead of perpetrating it. To break this chain and be inherently polite and kind towards all others involved in this value chain, we must first understand the circumstances most people in the Steel industry work in.

In India, most of the Steel, at least 60- 70%, is produced in areas where the temperatures are anywhere between 42 degrees centigrade to 50 degrees celsius. These temperatures are already pretty high. Now imagine all the heavy machinery and the furnaces in the steel plants that operate at 1500 degrees to 1800 degrees centigrade, and this heat radiates out into the working environment. Mind-boggling, isn't it?

It is little wonder then that the people working so hard in this heavy and hot process and environment tend to show behavioral changes such as irritability, frustration, aggression etc., over a period of time.

On top of these tough working conditions, most of the time, these people feel underappreciated and uncared for.

Remember this, these people are the core of your business, they are your most valuable human resource. First, make sure that their working environment is in the best possible condition within the limitations imposed by the nature of the industry.

Once you've ensured that their physical environment is at its best, irrespective of whether you are a producer, manufacturer or a business that performs value-addition, you must make sure to let them know that they mean a lot to you. And that you truly appreciate their services and genuinely care about their welfare.

As business owners, many times, we feel that the workers do not listen to us or care about us. However, I believe it is not so. This work is their craft, their profession and their bread & butter. Why wouldn't they care about it? Of course, they do, they care more than us. It's just that their environment and then feeling undervalued makes them behave in a certain manner.

If you make an effort to understand why they behave the way they do and make them feel worthy, dignified and appreciated. They will respond to you with immense loyalty and unbeatable productivity, and unimaginable profitability. As they blossom, your business will prosper too.

Another important part of the value chain are the drivers who transport the material in the industry. Steel loads are heavy, they are transported in special trailers that are heavy to drive and manipulate. No matter how sophisticated the vehicle, it is still a daunting task. Since they pick up the material from plants, consequently, they drive long distances in high-temperature areas. They crisscross across the country on long journeys, staying away from their families for long.

It is even difficult to imagine the kind of life they live, let alone live it. Ensure that your staff is always polite and courteous to them. Create a waiting/resting area for them in your facility with access to drinking water, tea and toilets while loading is going on.

It won't cost you much to be kind, but it will be extremely fulfilling and will go a long way in building goodwill for your business. Also, these drivers will never shy away from going the extra mile (literally) for you if ever needed.

Don't Forget your Suppliers & Buyers are Human too!

Now that we've talked about other components of the value chain in the industry let's not forget our buyers and suppliers; they are human too and need and deserve the same respect and courtesy as others.

Just being professional and ethical with our customers and delivering quality on time isn't enough. To be truly successful, we need to add gratitude and appreciation to the mix as well. The same goes for our suppliers. Yes, it's their job to supply us with quality material on time, but let's not take them for granted. A great trade secret is to actively appreciate them too.

Let me illustrate this with an example, when a supplier has delivered your material on time, don't just take it for granted. Call them and appreciate that you were able to deliver on time because they kept their commitment. Remember, you are only as good as your suppliers and are nothing without them. This person will never forget your gesture and will always support you with quality, on-time delivery and the best rates no matter what the circumstances. They will be your ally forever.

Similarly, let's say a customer pays you on time, don't just think that they owed it to you anyway, and it's no big deal. Make it a point to call them and thank them for how their paying on time helps with the cash cycle and liquidity of the business. And trust me, they will never forget this call, and you will always be their first choice, and a small humane gesture will win you a customer for life.

Another important thing I'd like to mention here is that we all want the best material at the best prices in the least possible time. This desire leads to a negotiation trail. Our customers negotiate with us, and we negotiate with our suppliers. Remember never to let things get heated up during negotiations, always mind your manners and your language. Handle negotiations both ways respectfully.

The Profitability Mantra

Never forget that we are all human, and all humans deserve to be treated with respect and care.

This mantra will win you many allies and long-term relationships that will foster goodwill and loyalty, leading to profitability.

Chapter 11

Coping with Price Volatility

Steel a Global Commodity

In this chapter, we will talk about the ever-changing prices of Steel, which can prove to be a real challenge for the players in this industry.

Historically and in the current perspective too, Steel has always been a commodity of interest globally and thus is a commodity that is being traded worldwide.

Steel is critical to many industries and plays a vital role in infrastructural development. Therefore, in addition to the regular trade players in the industry, even the governments of a majority of countries depend on this commodity a lot.

Being so widely used and critical renders the price of this commodity very sensitive to even small changes in various parameters. Hence its price is often volatile.

And because this is a commodity that is traded across innumerable exchanges and platforms globally, daily price variations in the price of Steel are the norm.

Keeping up and coping with these frequent, volatile price changes can truly be a challenging uphill task.

To understand what is causing these changes, how the market is reacting and when to expect them, you have to be constantly on your toes and be updated on the minutest of changes in the industry, minute by precious minute.

Watch Out, Mind It & Be Clued In

To be able to keep up with these volatile price changes, one has to keep an eye on multiple parameters simultaneously, as Steel prices are sensitive to changes on many fronts.

Political, economic, geographical and other day-to-day events affect and impact the price of Steel significantly. And remember these changes or developments need not necessarily be in your own area or country. Since Steel is a global commodity, an event in even a distant part of the world can impact the prices of Steel in your corner of the world.

For example, heavy rains in Brazil could lead to the temporary close-down of the Iron-Ore mines in Brazil, which would result in low production, causing lower supply compared to demand making the prices go up.

Or, say, another natural calamity in Australia that impacts the coking coal mines, leading to the rise in the prices of coal. This rise in coal prices will immediately impact the price of Steel and Steel products.

These are just some examples; any political event, such as a coup or change in government or an announcement of a huge project requiring big amounts of Steel etc., will all impact prices immediately.

Even policies on credit or other financial policies by the Reserve Bank of India will impact the prices of Steel, as will changes in oil/coal/fuel supply or prices.

Overall there are many parameters and indicators of the volatility of Steel prices, so if you want to make the right decisions and stay profitable, you will need to be super alert and have a birds-eye view of world events.

Being Innovatively Prepared is the Key

When your business is dependent on Steel raw material as a commodity, you will have to be innovative to be prepared to cope with the volatility of prices and remain profitable.

You must make sure to stay in touch with and speak to the industry professionals in all the sectors that impact the prices of Steel. Also, you must keep a watchful eye on the media and news, and basis the info gleaned from these efforts, you should make your judgements and decisions.

How I do, it is by talking to as many of my customers, suppliers/vendors and peers as possible. When you are in business, you will definitely come across a set of people who do deep and stringent analyses on commodity prices and movements of the stock market. Cultivate and keep in touch with such people and leverage the input given by them to make wise and profitable decisions.

Here's another tip that will serve you well; Keep an eye on the inventories and check how the global inventories are moving on a daily basis.

These are some of the shortcuts and super hacks to forecasting price trends so you can stay on top of price volatility in the Steel industry. I assure you that once you practice this, you will be constantly updated and clued in and will end up being profitable.

The Profitability Mantra

Always connect with customers and industry professionals and keep an eye on the media, world events and the stock market.

Ensure that you physically attend at least one industry event a month to interact with your customers, vendors, and peers to be updated on what's happening in your industry.

Also, from time to time, try to attend events from other industries. This will help you get a handle on the trends and forecasts of the economy in general.

This mantra will help you stay on top and be profitable irrespective of the price volatility in your industry.

In Conclusion

Friends, I have wholeheartedly shared with you all my learning and experience that I have gained over a significant span of time observing or being a part of the various aspects of the value-chain of the Steel Industry.

All that I have shared with you is born from experience and practicality; this is no textbook wisdom therefore, it will all be easy for you to implement. Also, I have ensured that what I have shared with you are small shifts with massive impacts. Therefore implementing these shifts will not prove to be disruptive or cumbersome to you or your operations.

The profitability mantras I have shared are guaranteed to give results without fail if you implement them in a disciplined and consistent manner.

Also, each of these tips, techniques and mantras will give you results individually, and you can start applying them as per your need, choice and preference in the respective areas and reap profitable results. However, when you work on all the areas by practicing what I have shared with you, you will see a massive wave of transformation.

This book is intended to be a personal guide, mentor or friend who has your best interests at heart and guides you every step of the way, so use it freely and keep going back to it when needed.

I would like to reiterate once again that everything shared here is simple but with great impact; the key lies in being consistent though.

So here's wishing you a journey of success with profitability and peace of mind once again.

I have guided you on to the path of success with ease through this book and you will notice the changes very soon.

However some of you will want more and more and more. For those of you who are hungry to scale up to the highest peaks, there are two ways of doing it.

Inspired by the success this book brings you, you can choose to scale up even further all on your own, figuring out the next steps yourself.

OR

You can choose to have me by your side and bypass the challenging cycle of hits and trials to scale up even further at supersonic speed with fast-track results.

For more details, you may contact me via

📞 Phone- 93028 34985

✉ Email- ankit.mehta@mehtasteels.com

CPSIA information can be obtained
at www.ICGtesting.com
Printed in the USA
BVHW061046151222
654216BV00010B/754